D1586578

50 Easter Things to Make & Do

Contents

Pecking hens

1. Fold a paper plate in half. Crease the fold well. Open it out, then paint the back of the plate, like this.

2. Fold the plate in half again. For a beak, cut a triangle from paper and glue it into the fold.

3. Cut some triangles from bright paper. These will be the spikes on top of the hen's head.

4. Glue the spikes to the back of the plate. Cut out circles of paper and glue them on for eyes.

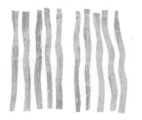 

5. Cut bright tissue paper into lots of thin strips as long as your hand. Gather the strips into a bunch.

6. Twist the strips together at one end. Tape them on for a tail. Rock the hens to make them peck.

Bunny giftwrap

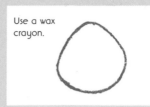

Use a wax crayon.

1. Crayon lots of heads on a large piece of paper. Leave spaces for bodies and ears.

2. Add two long ears to each head. Draw a small shape inside each ear and fill it in.

3. Using the same crayon, draw a fat bunny body below each head.

4. Draw two feet below the bunny's body, and a wavy tail on one side.

Draw a line to join the nose to the mouth.

5. Add two dots for eyes, an upside-down triangle for a nose and a curved mouth.

6. Add three lines on each cheek for whiskers. Fill in the bunnies with felt-tip pens.

Chick card

12

Crayon inside the corner, too.

1. Cut the corner off an old envelope. Crayon all over one side of the corner.

2. Take a piece of stiff paper. Fold it in half, then open it out again.

3. Glue the corner of the envelope in the middle of the card to make a beak.

4. Lift the top of the beak. Close the card and rub across it to flatten the beak.

5. Open the card. Draw a chick around the beak. Add some eyes, legs and feet.

6. Draw flowers around the chick, or glue on bright paper shapes.

Sheep and lambs

Use a fingertip to print flowers in the grass.

1. For the bodies, draw big and little wavy shapes, like these, on pieces of thin paper. Then, cut them out.

2. Dip the shapes into water. Shake off the drops, then arrange them on a large piece of paper.

You don't need to wind it neatly.

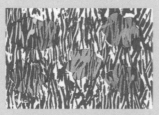

Make sure both pieces of tape are on the same side.

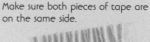

3. Tape the end of some yarn onto an old birthday card or postcard. Wind the yarn around.

4. When the card is covered, cut off any leftover yarn. Secure the end of the yarn with a piece of tape.

5. Paint the yarn green on the side without the tape. Press it all over the paper. Add more paint as you go.

6. Gently peel off the paper bodies. When the paint is dry, add faces and legs with paint or a thick felt-tip pen.

15

Rabbit face

 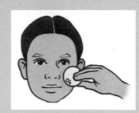 

1. Pour a little water onto a sponge so that it is damp. Rub the sponge lightly over lilac face paint.

2. Dab the sponge onto one cheek and twist it a little. Lift your hand and dab it on again.

3. Dab the face paint over the cheeks, nose and chin. Leave a bare patch around the mouth.

 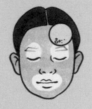 

4. Continue dabbing paint onto the forehead, leaving bare patches around the eyes.

5. With closed eyes and mouth, carefully dab white face paint onto the bare patches.

6. Sponge darker lilac face paint on the cheeks and forehead. Brush on pink eyebrows.

  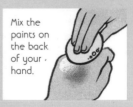

7. Dip the brush in the pink face paint again and carefully paint the tip of the nose, like this.

8. Paint a line from the nose to the top lip. Fill in the bottom lip. Add teeth, dots and whiskers.

Mix the paints on the back of your hand.

If you don't have lilac face paint, make it by mixing red and blue face paint, then adding a little white.

17

Potato print chicks

1. Lay lots of paper towels onto a thick pile of old newspapers.

2. Pour some bright yellow paint on top. Spread it with the back of a spoon.

3. Cut a potato in half. Then, cut away the two sides, like this, to make a handle.

4. Dip the flat side of the potato into the paint. Press it firmly onto some paper.

5. Cut a triangle from bright orange or red paper and glue it onto the side of the body.

6. When the paint is dry, add an eye, wings, a tail and some feet with a black pen.

Big flower prints

1. For a primrose, spread yellow paint onto newspaper. Cut a pear in half. Press it into the paint.

2. Print a pear shape onto some paper for a petal. Put a bottle top at the pointed end of the shape.

3. Print more petals around the bottle top. Dip the pear in the paint each time you do a print.

This will make a leaf shape.

Bend the cardboard slightly.

4. Lift off the bottle top. Dip a fingertip into green paint and print dots in the middle of the petals.

5. Cut a little potato in half. Dip it in green paint. Press it onto the paper around the flower.

6. For a bluebell stalk, make prints with the edge of a long piece of cardboard dipped in green paint.

Use the other half of the potato.

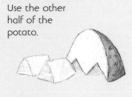

7. Dip a smaller piece of cardboard into the green paint. Do several prints along the stalk.

8. Cut the spare half of the potato in half. Use a knife to cut a zigzag carefully along the straight edge.

9. Dip the potato into light blue paint and print a bluebell flower on the end of each stalk.

21

Bunny napkin rings

 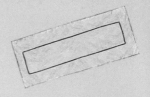

1. Fold a stiff piece of paper, the length of your hand, in half. Draw half the shape of a bunny's head.

2. Cut around the shape of the head. Open out the paper and use felt-tip pens to draw a face.

3. For the body, draw a rectangle on a piece of stiff paper twice the length of your hand.

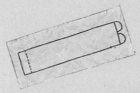 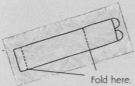 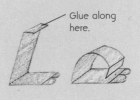

Glue along here.

Fold here.

4. Add two bumps at one end for the feet. Draw a dotted line a little way in from the other end.

5. Draw another line about a hand's length along. Cut out the shape. Fold it along the dotted lines.

6. Put some glue along the short edge and curve the paper over. Stick the edge behind the feet.

To bend a bunny's ear, roll it around a pencil.

7. Turn the head over and put two blobs of glue below the ears. Press the head onto the body.

8. For a tail, pull a piece off a cotton ball. Roll it into a ball and glue it on the back of the body.

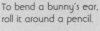

23

Surprise eggs

You could fingerprint flowers on the carton.

Glue on sequins if you like.

24

 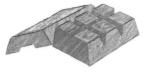

Use a spoon.

1. Trim any rough edges from around a cardboard egg carton. Paint the inside brightly.

2. Turn the carton upside-down and paint the outside with the same paint. Leave it to dry.

3. Gently crack the pointed end of an egg. Pull off the broken shell pieces. Pour out the inside.

4. Wash the empty shell. Leave it upside-down to dry. Crack and clean five more eggs.

5. Make bright patterns on the eggshells using crayons, felt-tip pens or food dyes.

6. Put a small Easter gift inside each eggshell. Carefully place the eggs into the carton.

You could put a little Easter egg or toy inside each eggshell.

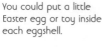

7. Fold small pieces of bright cardboard in half. Draw half a butterfly on each piece. Cut them out.

8. Close the egg box and tie a ribbon around it. Open out the butterflies. Glue them onto the box.

25

Dotty flowerpots

For an Easter present, you could plant some spring flowers in your pot.

26

1. Cut two strips of masking tape and press them on either side of a terracotta pot.

2. Cut two more strips and press them onto the pot. Press the ends inside the pot, like this.

3. Cut more strips of masking tape and press them between the other strips. Add more if there's space.

Scrunch up the paper towel.

You can wash the paint off the eraser, later.

4. Put a little acrylic paint onto a saucer. Dip a paper towel into it and dab it between the strips.

5. Fill in between all the strips of tape with paint. Let the paint dry, then peel off the tape.

6. Spread different paint onto a paper towel, then dip an eraser on the end of a pencil into it.

7. Firmly press the eraser onto the pot. Make a circle of dots for the petals of a flower, like this.

8. Wash the eraser, then dip it into a different shade. Add a middle to each flower, like this.

27

Hatching chick card

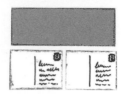

1. Take a piece of stiff paper. Cut it to the length of two postcards.

2. Fold the paper in half, short sides together. Open the paper out.

3. Fold the short sides in, so that they meet at the middle fold. Crease the folds.

Make the egg slightly smaller than the card.

Glue the egg across the middle of the card.

Don't cut the back of the card.

4. Draw an egg on the back of some giftwrap, then cut it out.

5. Carefully glue the egg onto the card. Draw a zigzag from top to bottom.

6. Pull the front and back apart carefully, then cut along the zigzag.

7. Draw a chick shape on yellow paper. Cut it out. Add a beak and eyes.

8. Carefully glue the paper chick over the fold in the middle of the card.

9. Draw legs with a felt-tip pen. Then, decorate the inside of the card.

29

Cress egg-heads

Cut out paper ears and glue them on for an Easter bunny.

Cut out a beak and wings and glue them on for a chick.

30

Use a spoon to crack the egg.

1. Crack the pointed end of an egg. Pull off the pieces of broken shell and pour out the inside.

2. Carefully wash the empty shell under cold water, then leave it upside down to dry.

3. Fill the egg with cotton balls. Pour in water. Tip the egg so that any excess water drains out.

4. Put the egg into an egg carton. Sprinkle it with half a teaspoon of cress or mustard seeds.

5. Put the egg in a light place. Add a little water every day. The cress will grow in 7-8 days.

6. Cut a narrow strip from the short side of a postcard. Bend it around. Overlap the ends and tape them.

7. Carefully stand the egg on top of the cardboard. Add a face using felt-tip pens and paper.

31

Marzipan chicks

1. Unwrap a block of marzipan* and cut it in half. Put one half in a small bowl and add about 12 drops of yellow food dye.

2. Mix the dye in with your fingers until the marzipan is completely yellow. Then, carefully cut the piece of marzipan in half.

Keep this piece for the wings. ——

3. Put one half in a bowl and mix in a drop of red food dye. If the marzipan isn't bright orange, add another drop of red.

4. Cut the yellow marzipan into five pieces. Make four of them into balls. Then, squeeze them at one end to make tear shapes.

Press in two eyes with a toothpick.

5. Make eight small yellow wings and press two onto each body. Then, roll a beak from the orange marzipan and press it on.

6. For the feet, make a tiny orange ball and flatten it. Cut the shape halfway across and open it out. Press a chick on top.

*Marzipan contains ground nuts, so don't give these to anyone who is allergic to nuts.

33

Boxes and tags

Put chocolates or other treats into a bunny box as an Easter gift.

34

Bunny boxes

1. For a gift box, carefully cut the top off a tissue box. Paint the box. Find a piece of thick paper the same shade and fold it in half.

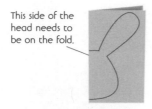

This side of the head needs to be on the fold.

2. Draw half of a bunny's head, like this. Keeping the paper folded, cut out the shape. Open out the paper and flatten it.

3. Draw a face. Then, glue the head onto one end of the box. Glue a cotton ball onto the opposite end, for a tail.

Easter tags

1. For a tag, draw a square on a piece of white cardboard with a wax crayon. Then, use a yellow crayon to draw a chick, flower or egg.

The crayon lines will show through the paint.

2. Use a different crayon to draw the details, like the chick's eye or the pattern on the egg. Paint over the picture with runny paint.

3. When the paint is dry, cut around the square, leaving a painted edge. Tape a piece of gift ribbon to the back of the tag.

35

Hen and chicks

The grass, fence and sky were made first and the hens and chicks glued on top.

36

1. Pull out pages from old magazines with brown, red, yellow and orange pictures on them.

2. Use a pencil to draw a big body, shaped like this, on red or brown paper. Cut around it.

3. Glue the body onto a piece of white paper. Cut out a wing from brown paper and glue it on.

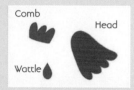  

Comb

Head

Wattle

4. Cut out a red crown for the hen's comb, a teardrop for her wattle and a large brown head.

5. Glue the comb and the wattle onto the back of the head. Glue on the head, overlapping the body.

6. Cut out and glue on yellow feet. Cut out brown feather shapes. Glue them at the top of the legs.

You could make a chick breaking out of an eggshell, like this.

7. Cut out and glue on white and black circles for the eye. Cut out a yellow beak and glue it on.

8. For a chick, cut out a yellow body, a paler yellow wing, orange feet, an eye and a little red beak.

37

Easter egg cards

1. Dip a thick paintbrush into water. Brush the water all over a piece of thick white paper.

2. While the paper is wet, blob different shades of paint onto it. The paints will run into each other.

3. Cut a rectangle from a piece of thick paper. Fold the paper in half to make a card.

4. Cut four small squares, the same size, from white paper. Glue them on the card, like this.

5. Cut four more squares from tissue paper, smaller than the white squares. Glue them on top.

6. Cut four egg shapes from the painted paper and glue them on top of the squares.

You could decorate the tags and cards with sequins, bows and glitter.

7. For a gift tag, punch a hole in the top of a big egg shape. Thread some ribbon through.

39

Tissue flowers

You could use these ideas to decorate an Easter card.

40

Draw slightly outside of the pencil lines.

1. Use a pink pencil to draw a stalk with two leaves. Then, draw a big oval at the top with lots of small petals around it.

2. Lay some green tissue paper over the stalk and draw around it. Then, draw around the leaves in the same way. Cut them out.

3. Lay pink tissue paper over the oval. Draw around it and cut it out. Then, draw around the petals on yellow paper and cut them out.

4. Brush white glue over the pencil stalk and lay the tissue paper stalk on top. Then, brush some more glue over the top.

The petals will overlap.

5. Then, glue on the leaves, petals and oval. Cut out some little circles of tissue paper and glue them in the middle of the flower.

6. To make a tulip, draw a stalk and leaves. Then, draw a flower shape, like this. Glue on a tissue paper stalk, leaves and three big petals.

41

Decorated eggs

You don't need the yolk and egg white.

1. Crack an egg on the rim of a mug. Then, carefully break the egg in half over the mug.

2. Wash the eggshells and leave them to dry. Brush white glue along the cracked edge of one half.

3. Fit the other half on top. Brush glue around the crack to seal it. Put it in an egg carton to dry.

4. Rip some tissue paper into small pieces. Then, brush the top half of the egg with white glue.

5. Press the pieces of paper onto the wet glue. Add more glue and paper until the top is covered.

6. When the glue is dry, cover the bottom half with tissue paper in the same way. Leave it to dry.

Decorate one side first, then let it dry.

Make up patterns of your own or use the ideas below.

7. Mix some paint with a little white glue. Paint one half of the egg. When it is dry, paint the rest.

8. When the paint is dry, mix other paints with glue. Decorate your egg with flowers and spots.

43

Easter garland

1. Pressing lightly with a pencil, draw a hen on some tissue paper. Use an orange pencil to fill in the comb and beak.

2. Lay the tissue paper on a piece of plastic foodwrap. Then, brush white glue around the outline of the hen's body and beak.

Only glue on the ends of the loop.

3. Cut a long piece of thread and press it into the glue. Cut another piece and make a loop. Then, glue the ends onto the hen's back.

4. Glue pieces of thread onto the comb, beak and wing. Then, brush glue over the tissue paper and sprinkle glitter over the hen.

5. When the glue is dry, peel the tissue paper off the foodwrap. Cut around the hen, taking care not to cut through the loop.

6. Make more shapes in the same way. Thread them onto a long piece of string. Then, use small pieces of tape to secure them.

45

Fingerprint bunnies

You could fingerprint a bird's head and body, then add little prints for wings and a tail.

46

Mix the paints on an old plate.

1. Make two blobs of bright pink paint by mixing red and white paints. Then, mix more white paint into one blob to make it paler pink.

2. Dip a finger into the bright pink paint and fingerprint a body. Then, fingerprint a head on one side of the body.

Only press the top part of your finger onto the paper.

3. Use your little finger to fingerprint the legs. Then, dip the side of your little finger in the paint and print two long ears.

4. Using the paler paint, fingerprint a patch on the bunny's head, where the nose and mouth will be. Add a print for the tail, too.

5. When the paint is dry, draw a cheek using a pink felt-tip pen. Draw shapes inside the ears and around the legs. Add lines for claws.

6. Use a black felt-tip pen to add dots for eyes. Draw a round nose and add curves for a smiling mouth. Then, draw lines for whiskers.

47

Egg toppers

48

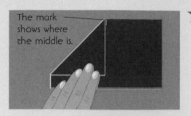

The mark shows where the middle is.

1. For a pirate hat, cut a piece of paper 15 x 10cm (6 x 4in). Fold it in half so that the short sides are together and the fold is at the top.

2. Bend the paper in half and pinch the corner to make a mark. Then, unfold the paper and fold the corners into the middle, like this.

You only need one half for the hat.

3. Fold up the top layer of paper at the bottom of the hat. Then, turn the hat over and fold the paper on that side up in the same way.

4. For a pointed hat, lay a small plate on a piece of paper. Draw around it. Cut out the circle and fold it in half. Then, cut along the fold.

Make all the triangles the same size.

5. Bend the paper around so that the corners overlap and make a cone. Then, secure the edges with small pieces of sticky tape.

6. For a crown, cut a paper strip that will fit around an egg. Cut out triangles along the top. Bend the paper around and tape the ends.

49

Springtime sheep

50

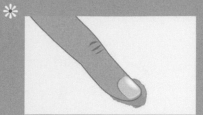

Dip your finger into the paint a few times as you print the body.

1. Mix a little red paint with white paint. Then, dip your finger into the paint and make a print for a sheep's head on some paper.

2. Wash your finger, then dip it into some white paint. Print a tuft of hair on top of the head, then make lots of prints for the body.

3. When the paint is dry, use a paintbrush to add white dots for eyes. Then, using a yellow crayon, draw lines under the body for legs.

4. Draw around the tuft of hair with a black pen. Add ears and a face. Then, draw around the legs, and add hooves and a tail.

5. For a butterfly, print four dots with your little finger. Draw a crayon line along the middle and add black lines for the wings and feelers.

51

Chirpy chicks

You could decorate an Easter card with some of these chicks.

52

1. Draw a circle with yellow or orange chalk or a chalk pastel and fill it in. Then, smudge the chalk a little with your fingertip.

2. Use a pencil to draw little lines around the edge of the chick for fluffy feathers. Then, draw two small dots for eyes.

3. Draw a triangle for the beak and fill it in with a red pencil. Draw two legs with three lines for each foot. Then, add wings.

4. For a chick in a nest, draw lines underneath the chick instead of legs. Then, draw smaller lines that crisscross at each side.

You could draw a chick pecking at some corn.

5. For a flying chick, draw two wings at the top of the body and a beak at one side. Draw two legs on the other side and add an eye.

53

Spring flowers

54

Draw on thick paper.

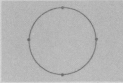

Hold the scissors so that the blades are together.

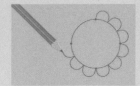

1. Draw around a small lid. Make a dot at the top, bottom, and on either side of the circle.

2. Draw three petals between each dot. Try to make all the petals the same size. Cut out the flower.

3. Pressing hard, run the tip of a closed pair of scissors along the middle of each petal to score a line.

4. Erase all the pencil lines. Gently pinch together the edges of each petal along the scored line.

5. Scrunch scraps of tissue paper into balls. Dip them in white glue. Roll them between your fingers.

6. While the glue is still wet, roll the balls in some glitter. Glue them in the middle of the flower.

This will be the stalk.

Curve up the edges of the leaf in the same way as the petals.

7. Cut a long strip of thick paper. Fold one edge into the middle and the other on top. Glue them together.

8. Fold a small piece of paper in half. Draw half a leaf against the fold and cut the shape out.

9. Unfold the leaf and glue it onto the stalk. Then, tape the stalk onto the back of the flower.

55

Springtime chicks

56

Draw on thick paper.

1. Use a pink wax crayon to draw a tree trunk and branches. Draw a big oval for the treetop.

2. Draw a nest in the tree. Draw the chicks' heads above the nest. Add their wings and bodies.

3. Use a purple pencil to draw two little triangles on each head for a beak. Add eyes and red cheeks.

Use a wax crayon.

Draw a worm in the beak.

4. For a mother bird, draw two circles for the head and body. Add wings, a tail and a tummy.

5. Use purple and red pencils to draw legs, eyes, a cheek and a beak. Add spots on the body.

6. Use a pink wax crayon to draw swirls on the trunk. Use pink and purple for leaves on the tree.

The wax resists the paint.

7. Use white and yellow wax crayons to draw flower shapes onto the top of the tree..

8. Fill in your picture with watery paints. Use a small brush to fill in details such as the leaves and chicks.

57

Easter crown

Make sure the
paper fits around
your head.

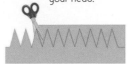

1. Draw a zigzag on a long wide strip of thick green paper, leaving a space at each end. Cut it out.

2. For the flower stalks, cut strips of green paper, taller than the height of the crown.

3. Draw flowers with five petals on yellow or orange paper, then draw smaller flowers with square ends.

4. Cut the flowers out. Glue the small ones onto the big ones, like this. Bend the little petals up.

5. Tape a stalk to the back of each flower. Tape the stalks in between the zigzags on the crown.

6. For bees, cut out bodies and wings from paper. Draw eyes and stripes on the bodies. Glue on the wings.

7. Cut out long thin stalks from green paper. Tape a stalk onto the back of each bee.

8. Tape the bees in between the flowers. Cut out flowers from white paper. Glue on yellow middles.

9. Glue the flowers onto the crown. Bend the crown around your head and tape it together.

59

Collage butterflies

These are for the butterfly's wings.

1. On a thick piece of cardboard, draw two teardrops, one a little smaller than the other. Cut them out.

2. Draw around the big teardrop twice on a piece of patterned paper or material, to make two shapes.

3. Draw around the small teardrop twice on another piece of paper or material. Cut out all four shapes.

4. Glue the teardrops onto some thick paper, with the big shapes above the small ones, like this.

5. Cut out a shape for the body from thick material. Glue the body down the middle of the wings.

6. Using a thin paintbrush, brush stripes across the body with thick paint. Add eyes and feelers.

7. Glue two circles of material onto the ends of the feelers. Glue a sequin on top of each circle.

8. Glue two more circles onto the wings. Glue stars cut from shiny paper onto the wings, too.

Tree decorations

Leave the
ends of the
ribbon free.

1. For a chick, cut six
strips of kitchen foil
about 45cm (18in) long.
Cut a piece of ribbon or
thread, too.

2. Fold the ribbon in
half. Tape it on one
of the strips of foil.
Scrunch the foil into
an egg shape.

3. Wrap another foil
strip around the egg.
Squeeze and press it
to make it into a more
solid egg shape.

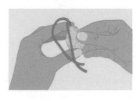  

4. Wrap the other
strips around the egg.
Press it until it is the
size you want your
chick to be.

5. Rip a piece of
yellow tissue paper
into small pieces.
Lay the chick on
plastic foodwrap.

6. Brush part of the
chick with white
glue. Press the tissue
paper pieces onto
the wet glue.

7. Brush on more glue
and press on more
paper until the chick
is covered. Leave it
to dry.

8. Draw on eyes with
a felt-tip pen. Glue
on wings and a beak
cut from yellow and
orange paper.

For an
Easter egg,
follow steps
1-7, using
different
shades of
tissue
paper.

63

Egg hunt

1. Mix some watery green paint and brush it all over a piece of paper. When the paint is dry, add some eggs using red and yellow paint.

2. When the eggs are dry, add extra blobs of paint to them. Then, use brown paint to paint a bunny's body, head and two long ears.

3. Paint smaller spots for flowers around the eggs and bunny. Then, use a darker green to paint grass in front of them, like this.

4. When it's dry, use a green felt-tip pen to outline the grass. You don't have to fit the painted shapes exactly. Draw lines for flower stems.

5. Use a bright pen to draw a flower on each spot. Then, draw patterns on the parts of the eggs that aren't hidden by the grass.

6. Use a red felt-tip pen to outline the bunny's head, ears and body, like this. Add small round paws and feet, and draw on a face.

65

Hanging eggs

Make the line thick.

Make the eggs different sizes.

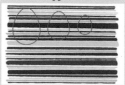

1. Pour paint onto a plate. Mix it with a little water. Paint a line across some white cardboard.

2. Add more thick lines with different shades of paint. Then, paint thin lines between them.

3. When it's dry, paint stripes on the other side in the same way. When that's dry, draw three eggs at the top.

You should have two eggs of each size.

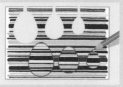

4. Cut out the three shapes, then draw around them on the striped cardboard. Cut these out, too.

5. Cut from the top to the middle of an egg. Cut from the bottom to the middle of its matching egg.

6. Push the slots together. Cut and slot together the other eggs, too. Then, cut a long piece of thread.

Press the thread down gently.

Use the loop to hang it up.

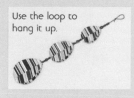

7. Brush a line of white glue along the inside of the largest egg. Lay one end of the thread on it.

8. When it's dry, thread on a few beads. Then, glue the thread onto the middle-sized egg.

9. When it's dry, add more beads. Glue on the last egg. Add more beads. Tie the thread into a loop.

67

Painted daffodils

The paint will run a little.

1. Use a paintbrush to brush water over a piece of paper. While the paper is wet, use watery yellow paint to paint six petals for each flower.

2. When the flowers are dry, use green paint to paint a thin stalk down from the bottom of each flower. Then, add long green leaves.

3. Use orange paint to make a cone shape in the middle of each flower head. It doesn't matter if the edges of the cones aren't straight.

4. When the paint is dry, use an orange pencil or felt-tip pen to draw a zigzag along the top of the orange cones.

You could paint lots of these daffodils on an Easter card.

69

Butterfly strings

Make the squares the same size.

Lay the square sticky side down.

1. Cut out two squares of book covering film. Peel the back off one. Lay it sticky side up.

2. Cut some thread into lots of small pieces. Cut out pieces of net, tissue paper and thin material.

3. Sprinkle the thread and material over the sticky square. Peel the back off the other square. Lay it on top.

Fold

4. Fold a piece of paper in half. Draw a little butterfly wing against the fold. Cut it out and unfold it.

5. Stick the wings onto the square with poster tack. Cut around them. Repeat this four more times.

6. Loop one end of a long piece of thread through a bead. Tie lots of knots. Trim off the short end.

Secure the small bead a little way above the big one.

Thread on more beads above the wings.

Sew through the bottom bead each time to secure it.

7. Thread a needle onto the thread. Push a small bead onto the needle and sew through it again.

8. Thread on more small beads. Then, push the needle through the middle of one pair of wings.

9. Add more beads and wings in the same way, leaving spaces of thread between each set.

Flower cards

1. Cut a rectangle of thin cardboard. Then, fold it in half to make a card. Rip a square of tissue paper and glue it onto the front.

2. Open the card. Lay it on a folded paper towel. Carefully, push a needle all around the edges of the card to make little holes.

3. Glue a square of patterned material about the size of the card onto a piece of paper. Draw a flower on the material and cut it out.

4. Draw another slightly larger flower on a plain piece of material and cut it out. Thread a needle. Tie a knot near the end of the thread.

Sew through the loop to secure the thread.

5. Push the needle through the middle of the large flower, then push it through the small one. Push a sequin and a bead onto the needle.

6. Sew back through the sequin and flowers. Tie a loop in the thread and sew through it. Cut off any hanging ends. Glue the flower to the card.

73

Leafy butterflies

Use the back of
the spoon.

Leaves with
veins that
stick out
make good
prints.

1. Put a sponge cloth
on an old newspaper.
Pour a little paint on
the cloth. Spread it
out with a spoon.

2. Press a leaf onto
the cloth, with the
veins facing down.
Press it onto a piece
of paper. Peel it off.

3. Make three more
leaf prints on the
paper. When they
are dry, carefully
cut around them.

Make the body
the same
length as
the leaf.

Leave the glue to dry.

These will be the feelers.

4. Cut a long body
shape from bright
paper. Glue the front
of a leaf shape onto
the body, like this.

5. Glue the other
three leaf shapes
onto the body so
that they look like
butterfly wings.

6. Cut two thin strips
of paper as long as
your finger. Roll up
the ends to make
them curl.

7. Tape the feelers
to the back of the
butterfly's head,
then turn the
butterfly over.

8. Use a felt-tip pen
to draw a mouth and
eyes. Decorate the
wings with stickers,
glitter or sequins.

75

Sheep card

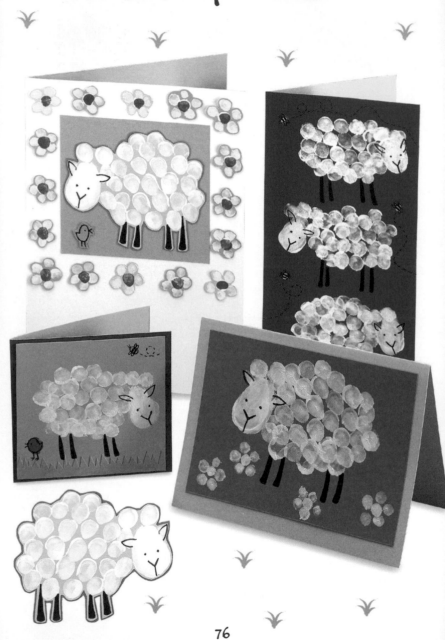

76

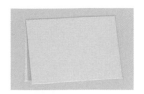 

1. Fold a thick piece of yellow paper in half, so that the shorter edges meet. Press along the fold.

2. Cut a rectangle of green paper, a little smaller than the card. Glue it onto the front of the card.

3. Put two paper towels on an old newspaper. Put white paint on one and yellow on the other.

4. Dip your fingertip into the white paint and fingerprint lots of dots onto the card for a body.

5. Dip your thumb into the paint to make a face. Add more fingerprints on top of the head.

6. When the paint is dry, use a black felt-tip pen to draw the sheep's eyes, nose, ears and legs.

7. Fingerprint little flowers on the grass with the yellow paint. Add white dots for their middles.

77

Butterfly card

The paint needs to be watery.

1. Pour some blue paint onto an old plate and mix it with water. Then, use a small brush to paint butterfly wings, like this.

2. Wash your brush. Then, while the blue paint is wet, dab small dots of green paint onto it. The green paint will spread a little.

3. Leave the paint to dry. Then, paint a dark blue body in the middle of the wings. Add thin feelers to the top of the body.

4. Paint lots more butterflies. Try painting orange wings with red bodies, and pink wings with yellow bodies. Then, leave the paint to dry.

Leave a white border around the butterflies.

5. Make your painting into a card by folding a sheet of thick paper in half. Cut around the butterflies and glue them onto the card.

6. For a splattered effect, dip a dry brush into some runny paint. Hold the brush over the card and pull a finger over the bristles.

79

Flower picture

The strips are for the frame.

1. Cut a rectangle of white tissue paper. Cut two cardboard strips, a little longer than the tissue.

Use a glue stick.

2. Glue the strips onto the sides of the tissue. Cut two strips for the bottom and top. Glue them on.

This will make a round flower.

3. Fold a square of tissue paper in half and in half again. Draw two curves and cut along them.

Rounded petals   Pointed petals

4. Repeat step 3 with more squares, drawing curves for rounded petals and pointed petals, too.

5. Open out all the flowers and circles. Glue the flowers onto the white tissue paper.

Glue more than one circle on some flowers.

6. Glue the circles in the middle of the flowers. You can cut out more circles for the middles.

7. For leaves, fold a strip of green tissue paper in half, twice. Draw a leaf shape and cut it out.

Use a black felt-tip pen.

8. Glue the leaves in between the flowers. Draw lines, spirals and petals on the flowers and leaves.

Painted flowerpots

Spotted pot

1. For a spotted pot, wash a terracotta flowerpot thoroughly. Leave it to dry out, then paint the outside with white acrylic paint.

2. Paint inside the top of the pot, too. Leave the paint to dry, then paint some light and dark purple circles on the pot.

Make the circles different sizes.

3. When the purple circles are dry, paint yellow circles overlapping them. Leave the paint to dry, then put a pretty plant in the pot.

Flowery pot

1. For a flowery pot, wash a flowerpot and let it dry. Paint it a pale shade. Cut some circles and petal shapes from different shades of thin paper.

Use a glue stick.

2. Glue some of the petals onto the pot to make a flower. Then, glue a circle in the middle of the flower. Glue on more flowers.

The glue is clear when it dries.

3. Paint a thick layer of white glue all over the outside of the pot, including the flowers. When the glue is dry, put a pretty plant in the pot.

Sparkly rosettes

The circles are for
the back of the rosette.

1. Cut five petals and
a circle from thin
cardboard. Cut five
slightly larger petals
and a circle from foil.

2. Glue a cardboard
petal in the middle of
a foil petal. Glue and
fold the foil edges
over the cardboard.

3. Cover the other
cardboard petals,
and the circle, with
foil. Bend each petal
to make a curve.

Use white glue.

4. Roll one end of a
curved petal around
a pencil to make it curl.
Do the same with the
other petals.

5. Dab a blob of glue in
the middle of the circle.
Press the petals, foil
side up, into the glue,
like this.

6. Cut three strips of
foil and roll them into
thin sticks. Wind the
sticks around a pencil
to make coils.

These rosettes were made
by adding extra petals
in step 5.

7. Tape the coils to the
back of the rosette.
Glue a small paper
circle in the middle
of the rosette.

85

Flower tiara

This will make a rose.

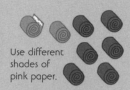
Use different shades of pink paper.

1. Cut a wide band of thin cardboard that fits around your head. Cut a little off one end.

2. Cut a strip of paper as wide as your first finger and twice as long. Fold over one end. Roll the strip up.

3. Let the strip unroll a little, then glue it to hold it together. Make eight more roses.

Glue two roses above the others.

4. Dip one side of a rose in white glue and press it onto the tiara. Glue on the other roses in a line.

5. Cut four dark pink and four pale pink strips. Glue the dark strips onto the ends of the pale ones.

6. Roll the strips into roses. Make seven tiny roses from small strips. Glue them all to the tiara, like this.

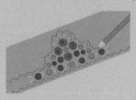

7. Make lots of small green rolls. For a teardrop, pinch one side of a roll. For a leaf, pinch both sides.

8. Glue the teardrops and leaves onto the tiara. Draw around the shapes, like this. Cut along the lines.

9. Cut halfway up one end of the tiara. Cut halfway down the other end. Slot the ends together.

87

Easter flowers

You don't need the lid.

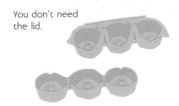

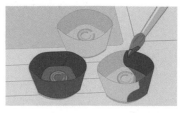

1. Carefully cut the lid off a cardboard egg carton. Then, cut the bottom part of the carton into two sections, along its length.

2. Cut one section of egg carton into three pieces. Paint them orange and let them dry. These will be the middles of the flowers.

3. Draw a petal on thin cardboard and cut it out. Then, draw around it lots of times on bright paper and cut out the shapes.

4. Turn the orange pieces over and glue the petals onto them, overlapping the petals a little. Then, leave the glue to dry.

5. Cut three pieces of yellow tissue paper. Scrunch them up, then glue them into the holes in the middles of the orange sections.

6. To make stalks, press a piece of poster tack onto the back of each flower. Then, press a green straw into the poster tack.

89

Sparkly tiara

This will be the tiara's head band.

Press down hard to make the band smooth.

1. Cut a wide strip of kitchen foil, a little longer than a pipe cleaner. Lay the pipe cleaner on the foil.

2. Squeeze the foil around the pipe cleaner. Roll it on a flat surface to make a thin band.

3. Cut five thin strips of foil, half the length of the band. Squeeze and roll them into sticks.

Tip off any excess glitter.

4. Cut out three four-petal flowers. Dab white glue on the tips and sprinkle on glitter.

5. Cut out three larger flowers. Dab glue on their middles. Press the glittery flowers on top.

6. Curl one end of each foil stick. Dab glue in the middle of the flowers. Press a stick onto each one.

Gently bend the sticks to make them wiggly.

7. When the glue is dry, lay the flowers glittery side down. Lay the head band on the stems, like this.

8. Bend the bottom of the sticks up, then twist them securely around the head band.

9. Twist the last two sticks onto the band between the flowers. Glue on sequins. Bend the band into a curve.

Spangly butterflies

You don't need this piece.

Put the wings shiny side down.

Fold

1. Fold some shiny giftwrap in half. Draw a butterfly wing against the fold. Cut it out.

2. Draw a smaller wing inside the first one, like this. Cut along the line, then unfold the wing.

3. Peel the backing off a piece of book covering film. Press the wings onto the sticky side.

4. Press sequins onto the film inside the wings. Gently sprinkle a little glitter around the sequins.

5. Press some more book film over the top of the wings. Smooth it flat. Cut around the wings.

6. Cut the short end off a drinking straw, above the bumpy part. For feelers, cut into the bumpy part.

Make sure the bead is wider than the straw.

7. Bend the feelers out. Lay the straw in the middle of the wings. Snip the end off, below the wings.

8. Tie a knot in some thread. Thread on a big bead. Thread on the straw, with the feelers at the top.

9. Glue the straw onto the middle of the wings. When the glue is dry, hang up the butterfly.

93

Bread shapes

94

1. Cut lots of shapes out of slices of bread using different shapes and sizes of cookie cutters.

2. Press a hole into each shape using the end of a straw. It's best to use a fat straw.

3. Lift the shapes onto a wire rack. Leave them overnight, until they are dry and hard.

4. Mix some white paint with white glue. Paint around the edge of each shape. Paint one side, too.

5. When the paint is dry, paint the other side. When that side is dry, use a pencil to draw on patterns.

6. Fill the patterns with different shades of acrylic paint. When it's dry, paint the edges.

7. To hang the shapes, push a long piece of thread through each hole. Tie a knot.

8. For a hanging chain, make two holes with the straw and tie the shapes together with thread.

95

Bunny in a burrow

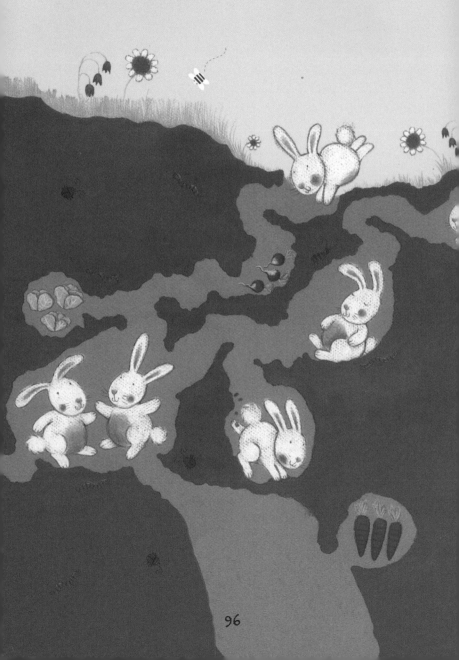

This will be the body
and the head.

1. Use a white pencil
to draw a circle on
some brown paper.
Draw an oval on
top of the circle.

2. Draw two ears. Add
shapes for the arms
and legs. Draw a little
circle for the tail. Fill
in the body.

3. Use a pencil to draw
around the head, ears,
arm and back. Add
little lines around
the tail.

4. Draw a curved shape
for the front leg. Draw
around the tummy,
the other leg and the
other arm.

5. Add dots for eyes,
a "V" for the nose,
a curved mouth,
whiskers and little
lines on the paws.

6. Fill in the nose
with a pink pencil
and add patches
inside the ears and
on the tummy.

7. Draw a wavy shape
for a burrow around
the bunny. Paint
around the burrow
with brown paint.

8. When the paint
is dry, use different
shades of pencils to
draw worms and
bugs in the soil.

Chalky sheep

98

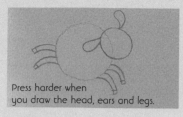

Press harder when you draw the head, ears and legs.

1. Pressing very lightly with a purple pencil, draw a circle for a sheep's body on pink paper. Draw the head, then add the ears and legs.

2. Draw lots of spirals all over the sheep's body, to look like wool. Then, draw a spiral at the back of the body, for the tail.

3. Use a darker pencil to draw a small "V" for the nose and add a curling mouth. Draw circles for the eyes, then add dots inside.

4. Use white chalk or a chalk pastel to fill in the body and tail. Then, smudge the chalk around a little, to make the edges blurred.

5. Fill in the head, ears and legs using purple chalk, then smudge it a little. Add white inside the eyes and pink dots for the cheeks.

6. Use yellow chalk to draw a line along the tummy and a smaller line under the tail. Smudge the yellow lines a little, too.

99

Flowers and bees

1. Using a wax crayon, draw a circle on a piece of bright paper. Then, draw petals around the circle.

2. Carefully cut out the flower. Cut out a paper circle and glue it onto the middle of the flower.

3. Make some more flowers with different shapes of petals. Cut leaf shapes out of green paper.

4. For bees, draw body shapes on yellow paper. Using a black crayon, add stripes and dots for eyes.

5. Cut out the bees' bodies. Draw a wing shape for each one on blue paper. Cut out the wings.

6. Glue the flowers, leaves and bee bodies onto a piece of paper. Glue a wing onto each bee.

101

Crayon chicks

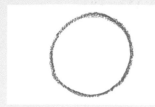

1. Use an orange crayon to draw a circle on a piece of paper. This will be the body.

2. Fill in the circle with a yellow crayon. Then, draw an orange beak on one side.

3. Draw an eye near the beak. Add a wing shape using an orange crayon.

4. Draw lots of orange lines for a tail at the back of the chick. Add two brown legs.

For a flying chick, draw the wings pointed up.

This chick has spiky feathers on its head.

Crayon butterfly

1. Fold a piece of strong, thin paper in half. Press along the edge of the fold, then open out the paper. Cut some cardboard into small pieces.

2. Glue the pieces of cardboard close together onto one side of the paper, like this. When the glue is dry, fold the paper in half.

3. Crayon over the top of the paper, using different shades of wax crayons. The shapes of the pieces of cardboard will show up on the paper.

4. Carefully cut off the crayoned part of the paper and fold it in half. Draw two butterfly wings against the fold, like this.

5. Keeping the paper folded, carefully cut around the wings and open them out. Then, draw feelers and a body on some paper.

6. Crayon the feelers and body and cut them out. Glue the feelers onto the body, then glue the body onto the wings.

Fingerprint flowers

1. Dip your finger into some purple paint and press it onto a piece of paper.

2. To make petals, fingerprint blue dots in a circle around the purple one.

3. For a rose, dip two fingers in different paints. Swirl them around on the paper.

4. Dip your finger in green paint and fingerprint leaves around the rose.

5. For a hyacinth, dip your thumb in pink paint and press it onto the paper.

6. Make more pink thumb prints underneath. Add a green stem with your finger.

Index

Written by Kate Knighton, Leonie Pratt and Fiona Watt.

Designed and illustrated by Josephine Thompson, Stella Baggott, Katie Lovell, Erica Harrison, Non Figg, Jan McCafferty, Antonia Miller, Amanda Barlow, Nelupa Hussain, Katrina Fearn and Andrea Slane. Photography by Howard Allman.

This edition published in 2015 by Usborne Publishing Ltd, 83-85 Saffron Hill, London, EC1N 8RT, England. www.usborne.com Copyright © 2015 - 1995 Usborne Publishing Ltd.
The name Usborne and the devices 🔍 🎈 are Trade Marks of Usborne Publishing Ltd. All rights reserved.
No part of this publication may be reproduced, stored in a retrieval system, or transmitted in any form or by any means, electronic, mechanical, photocopying, recording or otherwise without the prior permission of the publisher. UE. First published in America in 2015. Printed in Shenzhen, Guangdong, China.